Dinosaurs are split into two groups, ornithischian (bird-hipped) and saurischian (lizard-hipped).

Many prehistoric plants still exist today. Cycads, ferns, horsetails, and pine trees are all examples of these ancient and successful survivors.

Albertosaurus and *Tarbosaurus* were two large carnivores that had arms too short to bring food to their mouth.

An American Museum of Natural History expedition found remains of the *Oviraptor* in the Gobi Desert in 1923.

Eoraptor is recognized as the oldest known dinosaur—228 million years old!

Dinosaur eggs were found in 1922 when fossilized nests of *Protoceratops* were discovered in the Gobi Desert.

DINOSAUR MORE!

**To the Natural History Museum for all
the wonder and inspiration it gave a
small child, and to Arthur and his friends
at Sherborne Preparatory School, Dorset,
for their off-the-wall ideas and for the
use of their fabulous library!**

STERLING and the distinctive Sterling logo are registered trademarks of Sterling Publishing Co., Inc.

Library of Congress Cataloging-in-Publication Data Available

2 4 6 8 10 9 7 5 3 1
10/09

Published in 2009 by Sterling Publishing Co., Inc.
387 Park Avenue South, New York, NY 10016
Originally published in 2008 in the United Kingdom
by Ragged Bears Publishing Ltd., 14A Bennetts Field Industrial Estate,
Southgate Road, Wincanton, Somerset BA9 9DT England.
Text copyright © 2008 by Henrietta Stickland
Illustrations copyright © 1994 by Paul Stickland
All other illustrations © The Natural History Museum, London
Distributed in Canada by Sterling Publishing
c/o Canadian Manda Group, 165 Dufferin Street
Toronto, Ontario, Canada M6K 3H6

Designed by Karen Bale, Impulse Graphic Solutions Ltd
The moral rights of the author and illustrator of this work have been asserted

Sterling ISBN 978-1-4027-6494-3

For information about custom editions, special sales, premium and
corporate purchases, please contact Sterling Special Sales
Department at 800-805-5489 or specialsales@sterlingpublishing.com.

DINOSAUR MORE!

By Henrietta Stickland

Illustrated by
Paul Stickland

A first
book of
DINOSAUR
FACTS

STERLING

New York / London
www.sterlingpublishing.com/kids

DINOSAUR ROAR! was written to celebrate dinosaurs and introduce them to very young children. **DINOSAUR ROAR!** was a bit of rhythmic, rhyming fun, really! I discovered that nobody really knew what color dinosaurs were, so it was a wonderful opportunity for Paul (Stickland), the artist, to let his dinosaurs come to life in a colorful way. Now, some fifteen years after the first publication of that book, I wanted to explore some of our favorite dinosaurs in more detail. I hope **DINOSAUR MORE!** will inspire all you budding young paleontologists to start exploring the wonderful world of these extraordinary prehistoric creatures. If you're curious to learn more terms these scientists use in their work, check out the glossary at the back of this book.

DINOSAUR TIMELINE

How many millions of years ago did dinosaurs live?

227	205	180	159
Late Triassic	**Early Jurassic**	**Middle Jurassic**	**Late Jurassic**

CONTENTS

Dinosaur Long	Diplodocus	**6**
Dinosaur Fierce	Velociraptor	**8**
Dinosaur Spiky	Stegosaurus	**10**
Dinosaur Squeak	Compsognathus	**12**
Dinosaur Lumpy	Ankylosaurus	**14**
Dinosaur Roar	Tyrannosaurus	**16**
Dinosaur Slimy	Apatosaurus	**18**
Dinosaur Clean	Iguanodon	**20**
Dinosaur Slow	Triceratops	**22**
Dinosaur Tiny	Hypsilophodon	**24**
Dinosaur Fast	Ornithomimus	**26**
Dinosaur Strong	Giganotosaurus	**28**
Glossary		**30**
Index		**31**

144

Early Cretaceous

98

Late Cretaceous

65

DINOSAUR LONG

Diplodocus di-PLOH-de-kus

Meaning: *double beam*

Built like a suspension bridge, these improbably long creatures walked the earth during the Late Jurassic period. Huge muscles linked their pelvic bones to their tails. This helped them carry their tails off the ground. The length and size of the *Diplodocus* would make it very heavy, but part of the backbone was hollow, which would have meant that the *Diplodocus* weighed no more than two or three elephants.

Long, whiplike tail →

Scientists now believe the *Diplodocus* carried its tail in → the air. There are no fossil remains that prove otherwise.

DEFENSE

Like other sauropods, the *Diplodocus* would have traveled about in herds—it's much safer being part of a group! Its other defenses were a whiplash tail and an ability to rear up and use its front legs.

SEE HOW BIG I AM

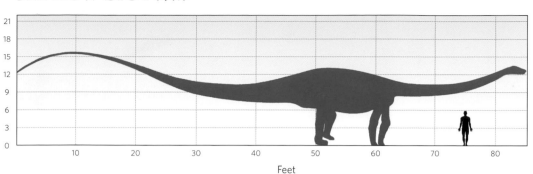

21
18
15
12
9
6
3
0

10   20   30   40   50   60   70   80

Feet

11 TONS

Bulky body ↓

Tiny head and small mouth with peglike teeth ←

← Walked on four columnar legs (quadrupedal)

Long neck ↑

DIET

The *Diplodocus* was an herbivore and had to eat huge amounts of trees, ferns, and other vegetation to keep alive. The *Diplodocus* only had teeth at the front of its mouth, so it was unable to chew. Instead it had gastroliths (stones inside its stomach) that helped grind up the vegetation. The ground-up food then passed to another digestive area, where it was further fermented by bacteria.

DINOSAUR FIERCE

Velociraptor vel-O-si-RAP-tor

Meaning: *quick plunderer*

This ferocious two-legged (bipedal) killer had large claws on its hind legs, with which it attacked its victims while holding them with its short, strong arms. Only about 6 feet, 6 inches in length, what the *Velociraptor* lacked in size it made up for with an aggressive nature. Fossilized remains have been found of this small meat-eater (carnivore) locked in battle with a much larger, horned dinosaur.

Velociraptors hunted in packs, picking out ill, old, or young victims.

SEE HOW BIG I AM

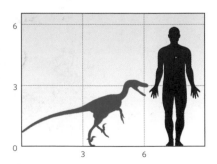

Feet

15-33 POUNDS

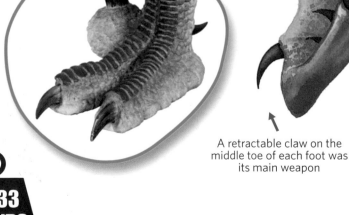

DIET

Meat and dinosaur eggs.

Three-fingered clawed hands

Approximately 80 very sharp teeth and a long, flat snout

A retractable claw on the middle toe of each foot was its main weapon

DEFENSE

Quick, sure-footed, and hard to outrun. Sharp claws and teeth for defense as well as attack.

8

DINOSAUR SPIKY

Stegosaurus STEG-oh-SORE-us

Meaning: *roofed reptile*

The *Stegosaurus* roamed the earth in the Late Jurassic period. It weighed about as much as a very large elephant, approximately two tons. The name *Stegosaurus* means "roofed reptile," which refers to the rows of bony plates on its back, neck, and tail. Some paleontologists think that the bony plates, which were full of holes and grooves, allowed blood to flow through and control body temperature. The plates were like prehistoric solar panels!

Large, flat, bony, triangular plates along its back, neck, and tail

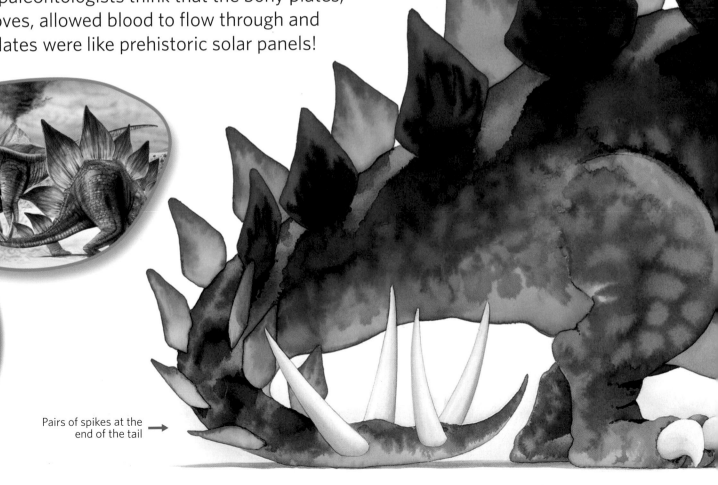

DEFENSE

The *Stegosaurus* was a very slow creature and could not outrun a predator. To defend itself it used a powerful tail, which was armed with bony spikes.

Pairs of spikes at the end of the tail

SEE HOW BIG I AM

Feet

Very small head with a tiny
brain and toothless beak

Walked on four legs (quadrupedal),
but its back legs were twice as long
as its front legs

2.5 TONS

DIET

The *Stegosaurus* was an herbivore and would mainly eat small shoots and leaves. The *Stegosaurus* had very small teeth and may have had stones (gastroliths) inside its stomach to help break up tougher plants.

DINOSAUR SQUEAK

8 POUNDS

Compsognathus komp-soh-NAY-thus

Meaning: *elegant jaw*

The *Compsognathus* was a small, agile predator that lived in the Late Jurassic period. One of the smallest dinosaurs, the *Compsognathus* ranged in size from a large chicken to a big turkey! Fossil remains of this dinosaur have been found in France and Germany.

DEFENSE

Speed!

Small, pointed head and sharp teeth

Long, flexible neck →

Three-toed feet with claws

SEE HOW BIG I AM

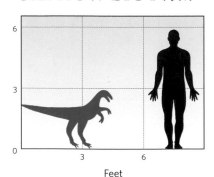

Feet

DIET

The *Compsognathus* lived on small lizards, mouselike mammals, and insects. Like all dinosaurs built for running, *Compsognathus* had long back legs (bipedal) that really helped cover the ground. This gave it the speed to catch prey. It is thought that the streamlined shape helped *Compsognathus* chase prey through the undergrowth.

DINOSAUR LUMPY

Ankylosaurus an-KIE-loh-SORE-us

3-4 TONS

Meaning: *stiff lizard*

The *Ankylosaurus* lived in the Late Cretaceous period, some 64 million years ago. This "armored" dinosaur could be as long as 33 feet from its head to the tip of its strong tail. It was covered with oval-shaped hard plates that were set into thick, leathery skin.

DEFENSE

When the *Ankylosaurus* was under attack it would have been able to stand its ground because of its protective thick armor. The *Ankylosaurus* would have used its heavy, clubbed tail for defense.

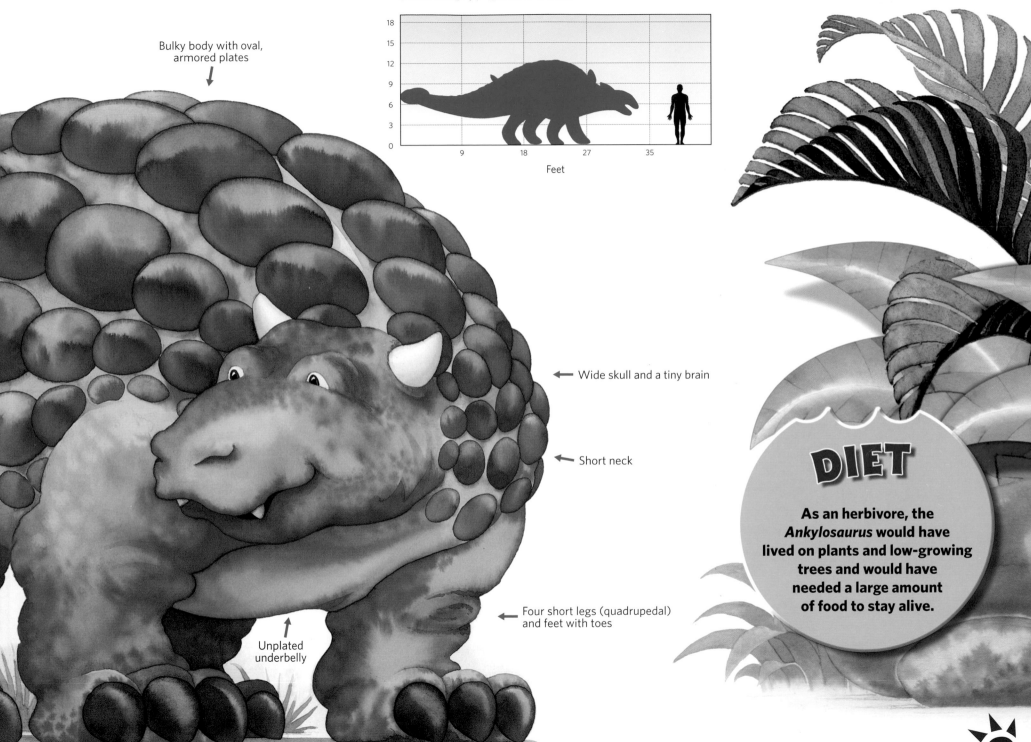

SEE HOW BIG I AM

Bulky body with oval,
armored plates

18
15
12
9
6
3
0
9   18   27   35

Feet

← Wide skull and a tiny brain

← Short neck

Four short legs (quadrupedal)
and feet with toes

Unplated
underbelly

DIET

As an herbivore, the
Ankylosaurus would have
lived on plants and low-growing
trees and would have
needed a large amount
of food to stay alive.

DINOSAUR ROAR

Tyrannosaurus tie-RAN-oh-SORE-us

Meaning: *tyrant lizard*

Aptly named, the largest carnivore ever was the *Tyrannosaurus*, which lived about 80 million years ago, during the Late Cretaceous period. This creature would have been fearsome to behold! Its massive jaws were filled with razor-sharp teeth around six inches long. These teeth had serrated edges to cut through flesh more easily. Fossil remains found in North America suggest that the *Tyrannosaurus* was about 20 feet tall and 39 feet long.

← Large, powerful jaws with long, sharp, pointed teeth

↑ Very short arms and hands with sharp claws

← Clawed feet

DEFENSE

Size and ferocity were the *Tyrannosaurus*'s greatest defenses. The only vulnerable *Tyrannosaurus* would have been an elderly or ill one, which could then fall prey to packs of smaller predators or scavengers such as the *Deinonychus*.

7.5 TONS

Large eyes

Huge head

Bumpy skin

Long, stiff tail

Long, powerful legs (bipedal)

DIET

Flesh, and lots of it! The *Tyrannosaurus* was a deadly and efficient killer. Over short distances it could move much faster than its prey. Some paleontologists believe the *Tyrannosaurus* operated through surprise attacks, charging at a victim in a short burst of terrifying speed.

SEE HOW BIG I AM

Feet

DINOSAUR SLIMY

Apatosaurus ah-PAT-oh-SORE-us

Meaning: *deceptive lizard*

The *Apatosaurus* belongs to the group of sauropods, which includes the *Diplodocus* and the *Barosaurus*. The sauropods were the largest animals ever known to have lived on land. The *Apatosaurus* existed in the Late Jurassic period.

The *Apatosaurus* had five-toed hands and feet and a big fleshy heel. The sauropods were so big, their arms and legs had to support the weight of about five elephants! Sauropods had very long necks and tails.

Like many dinosaurs, they were herd animals and would move around with their young close beside them.

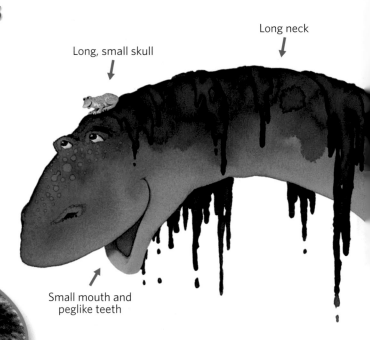

Long neck

Long, small skull

Small mouth and peglike teeth

Long, whiplike tail

SEE HOW BIG I AM

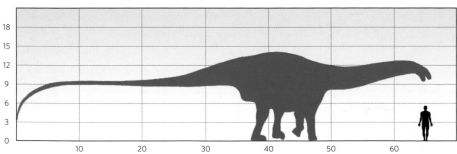

18
15
12
9
6
3
0

10   20   30   40   50   60

Feet

DIET

Sauropods were plant-eaters (herbivores). An adult would have to eat several tons of twigs and leaves every day to keep its huge body fed!

DEFENSE

While stamping its heavy feet, the *Apatosaurus* would use its long, strong tail as a whip to keep predators away.

33 TONS

Bulky body

Four columnar legs (quadrupedal)

DINOSAUR SLOW

Triceratops try-SERRA-tops

6 TONS

Meaning: *three-horned face*

Perhaps one of the most recognizable and best-liked of all dinosaurs is the *Triceratops*, which roamed what is now North America in the Late Cretaceous period. The *Triceratops* was the size of a very large rhinoceros and even rather resembled one. It had thick scaly skin, short sturdy limbs, and broad feet to support its heavy body. However, unlike the rhinoceros, the *Triceratops* had a large armored neck frill and three horns, not just one. A huge head made up one-third of its entire length!

Bulky, barrel-shaped body

DEFENSE

The *Triceratops* defended itself effectively with its sharp horns. It is thought that the neck frill could have acted as solar panels for warmth. Certainly it would have protected the neck and shoulders from predatory attacks.

22

SEE HOW BIG I AM

12					
9					
6					
3					
0	6	12	18	24	30

Feet

Large bony frill with pointed edges

Forward-pointing horns

Short, wide snout horn

Short legs with toed feet (quadrupedal)

Toothless beak

DIET

These huge creatures were herbivores. Like the *Iguanodon*, the *Triceratops* could chew well with its molars.

DINOSAUR TINY

Hypsilophodon hip-sih-LOH-foh-don

100 POUNDS

Meaning: *high ridge tooth*

Unlike other dinosaurs, the little *Hypsilophodon* had five fingers at the end of its short arms. No taller than a large dog, it lived in the Early Cretaceous period. The *Hypsilophodon* had sharp eyesight and a horny beak and stored food in its cheek pouches. The *Hypsilophodon* was bipedal and walked on its hind legs.

DEFENSE

Running away was its only defense. As a relatively small dinosaur, the agile *Hypsilophodon* could move very quickly. It usually moved around in a small herd, which made it much less vulnerable. To survive, keen eyesight was also essential—every second counted when running away from large predators.

Small skull, the size of a person's hand

Horny beak and strong jaws

Five-fingered hands

Long tail

SEE HOW BIG I AM

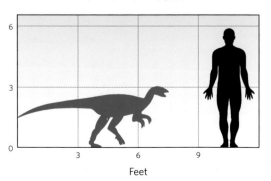

Feet

DIET

The *Hypsilophodon* was an herbivore and ate low-growing plants such as horsetails and ferns. Chewing vegetation would eventually wear down its teeth, but new teeth would grow in to replace lost ones.

DINOSAUR FAST

Ornithomimus OR-ni-thoh-MEE-mus

Meaning: *bird mimic*

The *Ornithomimus* lived in the Late Cretaceous period, around 70 million years ago. Bipedal and ostrichlike in appearance, this graceful creature could reach speeds of up to 45 mph over short distances, making it the fastest known dinosaur of its time. Its long tail would have stuck out as it ran, while its three-clawed toes would have dug into the ground and helped propel it forward. Fossilized remains of the *Ornithomimus* were first found in the United States (in Colorado and Montana) in the late 1880s.

Long, stiff tail

Three-toed feet with claws

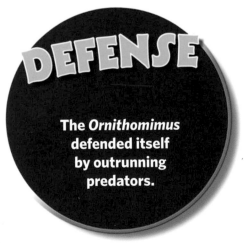

DEFENSE

The *Ornithomimus* defended itself by outrunning predators.

350 POUNDS

SEE HOW BIG I AM

Feet

Long neck

Toothless beak

Short arms with
three-clawed fingers

Long, strong legs

DIET

Some paleontologists believe that
the *Ornithomimus* was an omnivore.
If so, it may have lived on eggs, insects,
and small mammals, along with plants.
However, most paleontologists
believe the *Ornithomimus* to have
been an herbivore, because it
had no teeth—only a long,
toothless, horny beak.

DINOSAUR STRONG

Giganotosaurus gig-an-OH-toe-SORE-us

Meaning: *giant southern lizard*

The *Giganotosaurus* lived in the Early Cretaceous period and would have been even larger than the *Tyrannosaurus*, growing to 41 feet long. At first, paleontologists thought the *Tyrannosaurus* and *Giganotosaurus* were related, but further study revealed that even with many similarities, *Tyrannosaurus* and *Giganotosaurus* were completely different animals separated by vast geographical distances and also by around 30 million years (see the timeline on page 5).

Until 1994, when they found the first *Giganotosaurus* fossil remains, paleontologists believed that *Tyrannosaurus* was the largest meat-eating dinosaur ever!

Clawed feet ➔

DEFENSE

If you are a huge, healthy, meat-eating dinosaur with enormous sharp teeth, keen eyesight, and the ability to run fast over short distances, you don't need to protect yourself from anything—other than possibly your relatives!

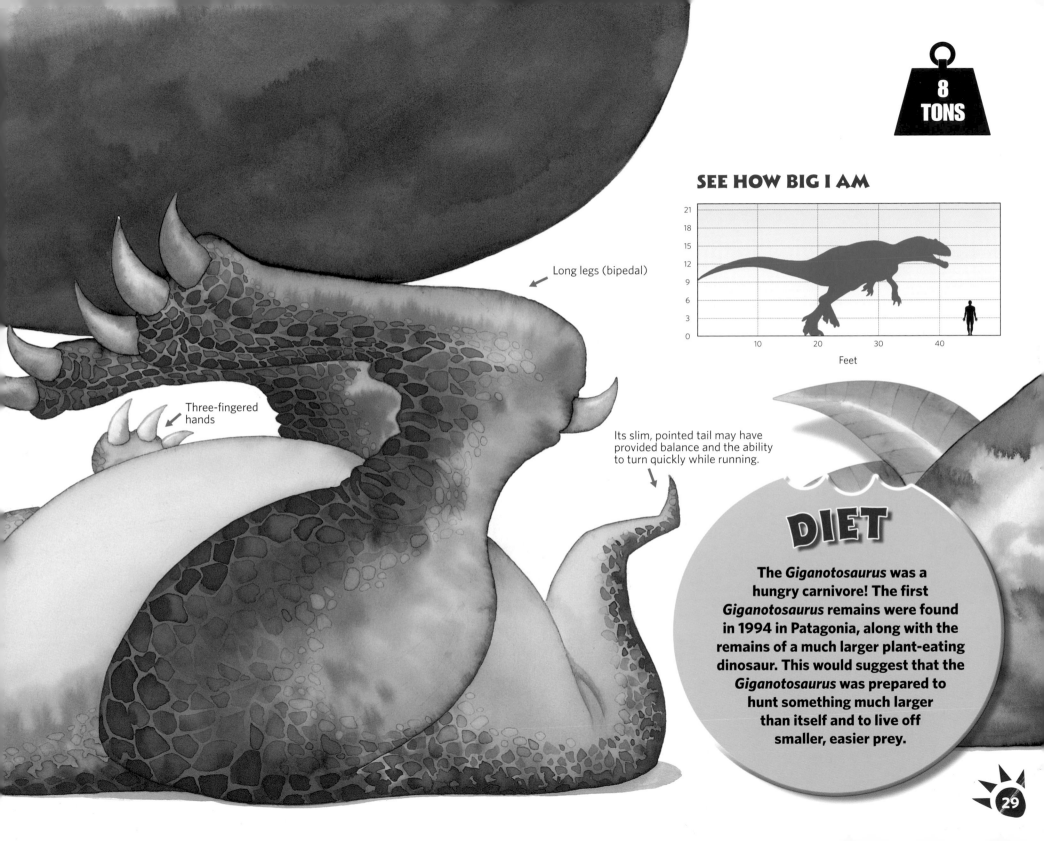

8
TONS

SEE HOW BIG I AM

21
18
15
12
9
6
3
0

10   20   30   40

Feet

Long legs (bipedal)

Three-fingered hands

Its slim, pointed tail may have provided balance and the ability to turn quickly while running.

DIET

The *Giganotosaurus* was a hungry carnivore! The first *Giganotosaurus* remains were found in 1994 in Patagonia, along with the remains of a much larger plant-eating dinosaur. This would suggest that the *Giganotosaurus* was prepared to hunt something much larger than itself and to live off smaller, easier prey.

GLOSSARY

aggressive
an aggressive creature is one that
often attacks or is easily made angry

bipedal
a creature that walks on its hind legs only

carnivore
a flesh-eating creature

defense
a means of resisting attack

ferocious
fierce or cruel

flourish
to thrive, to be successful

fossil
a relic or trace of a formerly living thing

herbivore
a plant-eating creature

gastroliths
also known as gizzard stones, these stones are held
in the stomach and are used to help grind up food

mammal
an animal that nurses its young

omnivore
a creature that eats both flesh and plants

paleontologist
someone who studies fossils

predator
a creature that attacks and kills other animals for food

penetrate
to find a way into something

prey
an animal hunted or captured by another for food

quadrupedal
a creature that walks on four legs

retractable
that which can be drawn up into the body (like a cat's claws)

sauropod
huge, long-necked, long-tailed, quadrupedal dinosaur

scavengers
creatures that seek and live off the remains of other
creatures' food or eggs

solar panels
a group of solar cells that absorb the sun's rays

vegetation
a mass of growing plants

vulnerable
capable of being wounded, open to attack

INDEX

Ankylosaurus	14	predator	10, 12, 19, 24, 26
Apatosaurus	18	prey	13, 16, 17, 29
bipedal	8, 13, 17, 20, 24, 26, 29	quadrupedal	7, 11, 15, 19, 20, 23
carnivore	8, 12, 16, 29	retractable claw	8
Deinonychus	16	scavenger	16
Compsognathus	12	sauropods	6, 18
Diplodocus	6, 18	*Stegosaurus*	10
Early Cretaceous	5, 20, 24, 28	*Triceratops*	22
Iguanodon	20, 23	*Tyrannosaurus*	16, 28
gastrolith	7, 11	*Velociraptor*	8
Giganotosaurus	28		
herbivore	7, 11, 15, 18, 20, 23, 25, 27		
Late Cretaceous	5, 14, 16, 22, 27		
Late Jurassic	4, 6, 10, 12, 18		
mammal	27		
molars	20, 23		
omnivore	27		
Ornithomimus	26		
paleontologists	4, 27, 28		

In 1992 a superb *Stegosaurus* skeleton was found, which finally proved that their back plates formed two staggered rows.

The massive head of the *Triceratops* was more than one-third the length of its body.

Unlike many other creatures, the *Tyrannosaurus*'s lower jaw was hinged halfway along so it could open its mouth extra wide—scary!

It is thought that the best armored dinosaur was the super spiky *Edmontonia*.

A Tyrannosaurus tooth could grow up to 18cm (7 inches) long.

All dinosaurs laid eggs.